Polygraph

Summer. Quebec City. Follow[...] woman, police suspicion rests [...] [...]nds, François, a student of political science. Meanwhile, a coroner conducts the gruelling autopsy.

Six years later, paths cross once again during the making of a film about the incident, triggering off a further round of unanswered questions and excavating the case – and its implications for those involved – anew.

Robert Lepage studied at the Conservatoire d'Art Dramatique de Québec and with Alain Knapp in Paris and subsequently worked with Ligue Nationale d'Improvisation and Théâtre Repère. Actor, director and writer, his international work includes his first solo show *Vinci* (best production, Festival de Nyon and Prix Coup de Pouce, Festival d'Avignon, 1987), *Polygraph* (*Time Out* Award, 1989; Chalmers Award, Toronto, 1991), *The Dragons' Trilogy* (Grand Prize of the Festival of Americas, 1987), *Tectonic Plates, Needles and Opium* (one-man show, Prix de la Critique Française, 1991), *The Seven Streams of the River Ota* and *Elsinore* (one-man show). He also directed the films *Le Confessional* (1995) and *Polygraph* (1996). From 1990 to 1993 he was Artistic Director of the French Theatre at National Arts Center, Ottawa and co-founder of Ex Machina in 1994. He was awarded the Chevalier de l'Ordre des Arts et des Lettres in 1990 and the Governor General's Award for Performing Arts in 1994.

Marie Brassard, performer and writer, trained at the Conservatoire d'art Dramatique de Québec and has since worked extensively in Quebec City, Montreal, Toronto and has toured Europe and Asia with some of Robert Lepage's productions. She co-authored and performed *The Dragons' Trilogy, The Seven Streams of the River Ota* and *Polygraph* (1990 Barcelona Critics' Award for best foreign actress, Association des Anciens du Conservatoire's Jean Doat Award) and performed in 'The Shakespeare Trilogy' (*Macbeth, Coriolanus* and *The Tempest*). She has scripted several short films, directed video clips for singer-songwriters and co-wrote the script of the film *Polygraph*, in which she played Lucie.

also available

The Seven Streams of the River Ota
Robert Lepage and Ex Machina

for a full catalogue of Methuen Drama titles write to:

215 Vauxhall Bridge Road
London SW1V 1EJ

or visit **www.methuen.co.uk**

Polygraph

Robert Lepage *and* **Marie Brassard**
translated by **Gyllian Raby**

Methuen Drama

Methuen Modern Plays

First published in Great Britain in 1997
by Methuen Publishing Ltd
215 Vauxhall Bridge Road
London SW1V 1EJ

Methuen Publishing Limited Reg. No. 3543167

The authors have asserted their rights.

ISBN 0 413 70720 2

A CIP catalogue record for this book is available from the
British Library.

Printed in Great Britain by Cox & Wyman Ltd, Reading,
Berkshire

Production History

Polygraph was first produced in French as *Le Polygraphe* at Implanthéâtre, in Quebec City, 6–14 May 1988 by Théâtre Repère. The play was developed through improvisation by actors Robert Lepage, Marie Brassard and Pierre Phillipe Guay, with contributions and script notation from observer-collaborator Gyllian Raby.

A second version was developed in Montreal for a November 1988 co-production by Théâtre Repère and Montreal's Théâtre de Quat'Sous. This substantially altered the original scenario through a process of improvisation-based creation by the actors and director during rehearsal, which continued throughout the run of the production.

The second version was translated into English for a production at the Almeida Theatre in London, from 21 February to 4 March 1989. Robert Lepage received a *Time Out* award for his direction. Since then, it has played under the English title *Polygraph*.

The following year, 21 February to 3 March, *Polygraph* was presented as part of the Harbourfront Festival's *QuayWorks* in Toronto. The script continued to metamorphose as a live, actor-created entity, with scripting and translation updates noted only periodically. In particular, the play became bilingual. The scenes between the Quebecois characters François and Lucie were played in French, with the introduction of projected English subtitles during scene nineteen.

Marc Béland and Pierre Auger replaced Pierre Phillipe Guay and Robert Lepage in the cast, and more fine-tuning alterations were made to the order of the scenes and segues between them. *Polygraph* featured at six summer festivals in Europe during 1990: Amsterdam, 12–16 June; Nuremberg, 19–20 June; Maubeuge (France), 5–6 July; Hamburg, 14–16 July; Barcelona, 23–26 July; Salzburg, 13–15 August. In Barcelona, Marie Brassard was given the Critics' Best Foreign Actress award for her portrayal of Lucie.

In 1990 *Polygraph* was part of the Next Wave Festival at
the Brooklyn Academy of Music, 23–28 October. Shortly
afterwards it played in the Studio season of Canada's
National Arts Centre (where Robert Lepage was Artistic
Director), and in April 1991 in Edmonton, Alberta as a co-
production of Workshop West Theatre and Northern Light
Theatre (where Gyllian Raby was Artistic Director). Since
then, the play has been touring around Europe in Brussels,
Glasgow, Berlin, Frankfurt, Vienna, Basel, Zurich,
Aarhnem, Paris, Dieppe and was last performed in Hong
Kong in February 1995. Other Canadian companies have
produced the play, and in 1996 it was translated into
Japanese by Kazuko Matsuoka, and with a Japanese cast, it
was produced at the Tokyo Globe Theatre by Robert
Lepage and Marie Brassard. In autumn 1996 a film version
was released.

Authors' Note

The three characters meet a few months before the fall of the
Berlin Wall. The murder of Marie-Claude Légaré took place
six years prior to the action, when François was studying
Political Science at the university, and David was in charge
of polygraph examinations at the Parthenais. The action of
the play occurs in 1989.

Lucie and François are Québecois, and so English is their
second language, but fluent, as it is also for David, an
emigrant to Canada from East Berlin; however, he has a
more 'perfect' command than they do.

David lives in Montreal but has not learned any French, so
constantly needs translations of menus, et cetera.

In the original production, all the scenes between François
and Lucie were performed in French, since it's their own
language. Lucie's theatre production of *Hamlet* is also in
French, as indicated in the script.

Translator's Note

I first translated *Polygraph* as it was being created, with the odd result that an English text existed before the authors considered their French production to be complete. Through the major revisions since then characters, time-frame and situations have altered – and in our separate reality the Berlin Wall has fallen. The living performance script has been allowed to metamorphose to reflect the authors' deepening perception of and relationship with their material.

Polygraph

Characters

David, *mid forties, German-born criminologist*
François, *late twenties, Political Science graduate and part-time waiter*
Lucie, *late twenties, actress*

Prologue

A brick wall runs right across the playing area, behind a shallow platform downstage. Music plays in a film-style introduction, while slides flash the play title and actors' credits in a large format that completely covers the wall. Then, stage right, a projection titles the scene, the film script-style introduction of each scene in this way will continue throughout the play. Dialogue and action begin during the projection of the credits.

Projection:
1. The filter

Stage left, in a 'flashback' performance at an inquest six years prior to the action of the play, **David** *reads a pathologist's report about a murder victim. He demonstrates his points by pointing at the anatomy of a skeleton which lies on the stage floor near his feet.*

Stage right, behind and above the wall, **François** *is in a Political Science class at the university, delivering a presentation on the Berlin Wall.*

David The autopsy has revealed that the stab wounds were caused by a sharp, pointed instrument which penetrated the skin and underlying tissues –

François After the fall of the Third Reich, little remained of its capital, Berlin, except a pile of ruins and a demoralised people.

David The body wounds are extremely large considering the small size of the inflicting instrument: I would surmise that the shape, depth and width of the wounds were enlarged during the struggle –

François The triumphant Allies enforced a new statute –

David – by the slicing action of the knife –

François – which split the city into international sectors: American, French, British –

David – as the victim attempted to defend herself.

François   – and to define their sector, the Soviets built a wall over forty kilometres in length, cutting the city in two.

David   The victim received cuts to the left hand, the right upper arm, and was pierced through the ribcage and the right lung, to the stomach. We have determined that the fatal cut was given here/

David *and* **François**   – Right through the heart –

François   /of the city.

David   – between the fifth and the sixth ribs.

François   The 'Wall of Shame', as the West Germans called it, was built to stop the human/

David *and* **François**   /Haemmorrhage –

François   /of Berliners leaving the East for the West –

David   – was caused by the laceration of the septum.

François   – symbolic of the division between the Communist and Capitalist worlds.

David   The septum functions like a wall bisecting the heart; it controls the filtration of blood –

François   For almost three decades, visitors from the West have been permitted to enter the Eastern Bloc –

David   – from the right ventricule to the left –

David *and* **François**   – but the passage is one way only. A sophisticated system of alternating doors open and close to allow the flow of –

François   – visitors from the West –

David   – deoxygenated blood –

David *and* **François**   – and to impede –

François   – inhabitants of the East –

David   – oxygenated blood –

David *and* **François**   – from circulating the 'wrong' way.

As if a continuous loop, the tempo of the 'filter' dialogue increases with the volume and drive of the music. As it is repeated, the naked body of **Lucie** *rises stage left behind the wall, lit by anatomical slide projections: muscles, veins, organs and bones superimposed on her flesh, as though she is transparent. The scene ends on a music crescendo and a brief blackout.*

Projection:
2. Parthenais Institute of Criminal Pathology, Montreal

Interior, night.

In the blackout, more meditative music plays. Lights reveal first the skeleton, which slowly rises to its feet, then the rest of the scene. Stage right, **David** *is at work, note-taking as he watches intently the bleeping, whirring Polygraph machine. He turns off the Polygraph, puts on his coat, and takes a letter from the pocket. He reads a few lines to himself then replaces it. Thoughtfully, he lights a cigarette. He approaches the skeleton and slowly takes its head in his hand, assuming the cliché position of Hamlet with Yorick's skull. Lights cross-fade to the next scene as* **Lucie**'s *voice is heard.*

Projection:
3. Hamlet

Exterior, night.

Lucie *appears above and behind the wall, stage left, reciting in profile Hamlet's speech to Yorick (Act 5, Scene 1). She wears black, and holds a skull.*

Lucie   Hélas, pauvre Yorick! . . . Je l'ai connu, Horatio! C'était un garçon d'une verve infinie, d'une fantaisie exquise; il m'a porté sur son dos mille fois. Et maintenant quelle horreur il cause à mon imagination! Le coeur m'en lève. Ici pendaient les lèvres que j'ai baisées, je ne sais combien de fois. Où sont vos plaisanteries maintenant? Vos escapades? Vos chansons? Et ces éclairs de gaie té qui

faisaient rugir la table de rires? Quoi! Plus un mot à présent
pour vous moquer de vos propres grimaces? Plus de lèvres?
... Allez maintenant trouver madame dans sa chambre et
dites-lui qu'elle a beau se mettre un pouce de fard, il faudra
bien qu'elle en vienne à cette figure là! Faites la bien rire avec
ça ...
[Alas, poor Yorick! I knew him, Horatio. A fellow of infinite
jest, of most excellent fancy. He hath bore me on his back a
thousand times. And now how abhorred in my imagination
it is! My gorge rises at it. Here hung those lips that I have
kissed I know not how oft. Where be your gibes now? Your
gambols, your songs, your flashes of merriment that were
wont to set the table on a roar? Not one now to mock your
own grinning? Quite chop-fallen? Now get you to my lady's
table and tell her, let her paint an inch thick, to this favour
she must come. Make her laugh at that ...]

*Lights cross-fade into the next scene. A change in soundscore now
suggests the hubbub of a busy restaurant.*

Projection:
4. François

Interior, night.

François *enters stage left with a 'table for two' over his shoulder.
This he swings down in an easy movement. Quickly setting it with
plates and cutlery, he then positions two chairs either side. When the
table is 'set' he immediately unmakes it, swings it over his shoulder, and
repeats the whole sequence in a different space, all the while talking
rapidly to invisible customers. During the course of the scene he covers
the whole stage, so suggesting a room full of tables, and he never stops
talking.*

François   Vous avez bien mangé? Je vous apporte
l'addition, monsieur. Par ici s'il vous-plaît. Vous avez
regardé le menu du jour sur le tableau? Oui. C'est pour
combien de personnes? Par ici s'il vous plaît. Prendriez-vous
un digestif? Deux cafés cognac ... tout de suite ... Ce sera pas

long, monsieur ... Oui, bonjour. Non, malheureusement, on
a plus de rôti à l'échalotte. A la place, le chef vous suggère son
poulet rôti, un poulet au citron, c'est délicieux. Alors, deux
fois. Allez-vous prendre un dessert? Aujourd'hui, c'est la
tarte à l'orange maison. Elle est excellente, je vous la
recommande ... Oui. Une personne. Par ici s'il vous plaît.
For two? ... I'm sorry we don't 'ave any English menu ... I'll
translate for you. Deux places? Par ici s'il vous plaît. Pardon?
Vous auriez dû me le dire, je vous l'aurais changé sans
problème. Oui, la prochaine fois, d'accord. Par ici s'il vous
plaît.
[Did you enjoy your meal? The bill? At once, sir. Would you
please follow me? Did you notice today's specials on the
board? Yes. You'd like a table for ...? Please, follow me.
Something to drink, perhaps? You'd like to see the wine list.
Two coffees with cognac ... It'll just be a moment, sir! Good
evening. No, unfortunately we're all out of the roast veal.
The chef suggests instead the chicken in lemon: it's very
good. So ... two chicken. Would you care for dessert?
Today's special is Homemade Orange Cheesecake; it's
excellent ... So, a table for one? ... Would you please follow
me ... For two? ... I'm sorry, we have no English menus, I'll
be happy to translate for you. For two, sir? ... I have one
table over there ... Sorry? Oh ... You should have told me
before, I would have replaced it, no problem ... OK ... Next
time ... This way please; a table for ...?]

Lucie *enters and sits at the table, talking rapidly to keep pace with his
non-stop work.*

Lucie   Salut, François! Aie, il parait que toi pis ton chum,
vous êtes venus voir la pièce hier ... Vous êtes pas venus me
voir après, est-ce que c'est parce que vous avez pas aimé ça?
[Hi, François! How're you doing? ... Hey, they said you and
your boyfriend came to the show last night? Why didn't you
come backstage to see me – you didn't like it?]

François   Ah non! C'était magnifique ... On a beaucoup
aimé l'idée de faire jouer Hamlet par une femme ... De nos
jours, c'est beaucoup plus percutant que ce soit une femme

qui tienne ces propos-là plutôt qu'un homme.
[No! It was excellent! We thought it was brilliant to cast a woman as Hamlet; some of those questions take on real significance coming from a woman; especially for today – more so than from a man.]

Lucie Ben, en fait, à l'origine, c'était pas prévu ... Ils m'ont téléphoné à la dernière minute ... Le gars qui jouait Hamlet est tombé malade puis le metteur en scène a eu l'idée de me demander de le remplacer ...
Aie, François, j'ai entendu dire ... Y paraît qu'à CKRL, ils cherchent un annonceur pour lire le bulletin de nouvelle le soir ... t'as une belle voix ... il me semble que tu serais bon là dedans.
[Actually, it wasn't planned that way, originally. They called me at the last minute. The guy who was playing Hamlet got sick and the director had this strange idea of casting a woman for the part.
Oh, François – I heard the radio station CKRL is looking for someone to read the late-night news. You've got such a nice voice, why don't you apply? You'd be great!]

François C'est gentil d'avoir pensé à moi, mais ces temps-ci c'est pas possible, j'ai trop d'ouvrage au restaurant.
[Thanks for thinking of me, but it wouldn't be possible right now. Too much work at the restuarant.]

Lucie Aie, j'ai croisé Alain dans l'escalier tantôt, il m'a même pas dit bonjour ... c'est tu parce qu'il est fâché contre moi?
[François, is Alain angry at me? I met him on the stairs at home, and he didn't even say hello ... what's his problem?]

François T'en fais pas avec ça ... c'est à moi qu'il en veut.
[No problem. It's me he's mad at.]

Lucie En tous cas, je te remercie beaucoup. C'était très bon.
[Ah. Well ... Thanks. It was great!]

Lucie *exits;* **François** *continues at the same pace.*

François A bientôt, Lucie. [See you, Lucie!]

François *goes out with the table settings, returns and sits at the table. Change in lights and music indicate that it is now the end of the day, and he is exhausted. He taps out three lines of coke and snorts it.* **David** *enters the restaurant over the wall, sliding down with his back to it, his arms and his suit jacket spread like a giant, ominous spider.* **David** *lands smoothly in the empty seat across the table from* **François**.

David
François, can you hear me properly?
But you can't actually see me, can you?
François, we are going to conduct a little test.
Are we in Canada?
Is it summertime?
Was it you who killed Marie-Claude Légaré?

François *shakes his head, as if to dislodge these disturbing thoughts and* **David** *disappears in a slow reversal of the way he came. Lights cross-fade to a spotlight stage right.*

Projection:
5/6. The audition/Sauvé Metro station

Interior, day.

Lucie *walks diffidently into the bright spotlight. She squints nervously at the light as she begins her audition, talking to unseen interviewers positioned in the audience. Her English is good, but sometimes hesitant and a bit convoluted.*

Hi. My name is Lucie Champagne . . .
My hair is shorter than on the photograph because I'm
playing a guy in a show right now, so they cut it . . .
I should tell you right away – I've never . . .
What? To the camera! . . . OK . . .

She turns slightly to face it.

I've never worked on a movie before – but I have done a lot of video, mainly comedies, but I like drama just as much . . . my videos were for the government social services . . . Let's see . . . an example would be . . . ?

Oh yes! I played a woman whose money was stolen by her brother-in-law; to you or me that might seem a pretty tame crisis — but for this woman, it was profoundly dramatic, I mean, it was completely devastating, because, well . . . it was her money . . . and . . . it was her brother-in-law . . . so I . . . I had to play this part with as much emotion as I possibly could . . .

Oh yes! While I was at the theatre school I was in a play by Tennessee Williams called: *Talk To Me Like the Rain and Let Me Listen*. It has a long title but the play is actually very short. It's about a couple, and I played the woman, and my character was anorexic. But not by choice . . . I mean, she was anorexic because she hadn't eaten for four days, because she didn't have any money, because her boyfriend took off with the welfare check; I loved that role!

My first experience? Well, I'll tell you, but you'll laugh! It was for the priest's birthday when I was in Grade One. Everyone in my class was in it. The other kids all lined up in front of the wall behind me, and they sang,

'Where are you going little Bo-Peep, where are you going Bo-Peep . . . ?'

And I was out in front wearing a little white dress, and I sang back. 'I am following this beauteous star and all my sheep are saying baaa . . . '!

My God, it was so great! I loved to tell lies when I was a kid — that is, I was not a liar but . . . I was fascinated that I could say untrue things but do it so convincingly that people would believe me; maybe that explains why I always wanted to be an actress . . .

What? Oh! Yes . . . For my audition I have brought a soliloquy from Shakespeare's *Hamlet* . . .

No, no, not the part of Ophelia, the part of Hamlet.

Oh . . . you would prefer an impro. Euh . . .

She looks around.

Should I improvise here? . . .

What would you like me to improvise?

To imagine myself in a tragic situation . . . ?

Is that so you can see if I can cry? Because, I mean . . . I can't

cry at the drop of a hat . . .
I mean, what I mean is: put me in a movie where there's a sad
scene where I have to cry, and I'd concentrate to the point
where tears would well up, but I can't cry just like that . . .
here . . .
To imagine myself in an absolute state of panic . . .
Don't you think I'm panicking enough here?
OK, I'll do it.

Projection:
Sauvé Métro

*The Metro station logo is also projected on the wall. The soundscape
evokes a large, hollow-echoing Underground.* **Lucie** *focuses on the
front edge of the stage, an expression of petrified horror on her face; she
backs up to lean against the wall with an inarticulate scream.* **David**
*enters. He kneels, expressionless, beside the 'tracks' at the edge of the
stage. In his hand he holds a bloody T-shirt, which he places in a zip-
lock plastic bag. He takes out a notebook and writes. In the meantime*
Lucie *is going into shock, shouting and crying in semi-hysteria.*
David *assesses her, completes his notes, puts away his notebook
carefully, then goes to her. As she sobs for breath, he pulls her away
from the wall to lean against him, and smooths her shoulders,
rhythmically. Gradually, she is able to control her breathing. He checks
her pulse, her heart-beat, and takes some pills from a bottle in his
pocket, which he offers to her. When he speaks, it is with a German
accent.*

David   Take this, it's a mild tranquiliser.

Lucie   Was . . . was he killed on impact?

David   Yes. Can I give you a lift somewhere?

Lucie   Yes.

David   Where do you live?

Lucie   In Quebec City.

David *is momentarily alarmed as it is three hours drive to Quebec City
from Montreal.*

Lucie   I was on my way to catch the bus.

David   I'll walk you to the bus terminal then.

David *puts his arm around her shoulders and they move off towards stage left.* **Lucie** *breaks away, runs back to look at the tracks, and then returns to her starting position in the present, leaning against the wall in her audition spotlight. As* **David** *exits, this is now the only light on stage.*

Back in the audition.

Lucie   Was that enough?

Blackout. A metallic, driving music accompanies a red light that shines from behind the wall.

Projection:
7. The Flesh

Interior, night.

François *enters, like a predator, over the top of the wall into a gay bar. He drinks a beer, watching bodies on the dance-floor. Soon he realises that he's being assessed by one of the crowd, and he agrees to follow the man stage right to a back room for sex. A change in light and baffling of sound indicate they are now private. In a very sensual scene,* **François** *takes off his shirt, and then his belt, which he gives to his companion. Their relationship is one where they 'play' at coercion.* **François** *unzips his pants and kneels facing the wall, supported by the wall. As we hear the sounds of the whiplash,* **François'** *body physically recoils against the wall with each blow. As he comes, as his body shudders, the wall bleeds, gushing blood.* **François** *meets the eyes of his lover. He gives a cursory wave as the other man leaves.*
With an air of soul-weary satisfaction, **François** *gathers his clothes, and returns to the bar. As lights fade to black, he drinks another beer and watches the dance-floor.*
In the blackout, a two-way mirror drops from the ceiling to hang above the wall stage right. It is the make-up mirror of **Lucie's** *dressing-room at the theatre. The audience watch the scene from 'behind' the mirror.*

Projection:
8. The tears

Interior, night.

David *is waiting in the dressing-room with a bunch of carnations, a flower associated with funerals and said by Québecois actors to bring bad luck to a show.* **Lucie** *enters, having finished her performance of Hamlet; she holds the skull of Yorick.*

David   Good evening.

Lucie   David, my God, it's you! Did you come all the way from Montreal just to see the show?

David   Well, in fact, I had some business this week in Quebec City, and since I promised myself I would see you act one day: here I am.

Lucie   We weren't exactly sold out tonight . . .

David   That makes it more intimate theatre.

Lucie   So, what did you think? Did you like it?

David   Well, I thought it was quite interesting. Oh, here!

He presents her with the carnations.

Lucie   Oh my God! Carnations! – Thank you . . .

David (*examines the skull on the dressing-room table*)   Is this Yorick?

Lucie   You know him well?

David   Of course . . . He is the only character who isn't killed at the end of the play!

Lucie   I like the way you call him by his name. Round here they just call him 'the skull'.

David   What is written on his forehead? (*Reading*.) . . . Hélas, pauvre Yorick . . .

Lucie   My lines! I didn't have time to learn them properly so I wrote them out . . .

Would you mind waiting for me, just a second? I have to get changed and I'll be right back.

Lucie *exits*.

David 'To be or not to be, that is the question . . . '. It must be difficult to pronounce 'To be or not to be', and to question the fundamental things of life: love, honour –

David *and* **Lucie** (*simultaneously, as she re-enters*) – death . . .

Lucie It's on my mind . . . more than ever . . . seeing that boy throw himself in front of the train in Montreal. You know . . . I want to thank you for driving me all the way back to Quebec City . . . you didn't have to do that.

David Let's just say I was not acting purely out of duty; it also gave me the opportunity to get to know you a little better and to make a new friend.
. . . So . . . What about the movie? Did you get the part?

Lucie Not yet . . . but next week they want me to do some screen tests. I'm terrified because they want to shoot a scene where I cry and it's not so easy to do . . . They gave me this.

She takes a tube from the dressing-room table.

You'll never guess what it's for. It's a special product they use in movies to help actors cry.

David Really! Why?

Lucie Imagine re-doing the same sad scene twelve times? It's hard to cry every time, right? So, they put this in the actor's eyes and the tears flow all on their own.

David Wait a minute. Are you telling me that when an actress like . . . Jane Fonda for example, . . . when she cries, it's all fake?

Lucie Sometimes, yes.

David What a deception! I believed that for an actor at least, tears were the ultimate proof of true emotion!

Lucie This is another of the misconceptions people have about acting?
D'you want to try it?

David Surely you don't want to make me cry!

Lucie Yes! You'll see, it won't hurt . . . It will be funny!

David All right then! What should I do here?

Lucie First, I'll ask you to take off your glasses. And now, since we are making a movie, I'll ask you to think about something sad, so the scene will be truthful.

David Something sad . . . Something recent?

Lucie Whatever you want!
And now I say:
'Quiet on the set . . . sound . . . camera . . . action!'

*As **David** remembers, there is a musical theme reminiscent of his past in East Berlin. **Lucie** freezes, still holding his glasses. Like a statue, she slowly recedes from the playing area, as if flying away. The set of the dressing-room disappears simultaneously, and a projection of the Brandenburg Door fills the cyclorama. **David**, in another time, brings out a letter from his pocket. A woman's voice is heard, reading the letter in German.*

Anna's Voice Ich weiss, dass man niemanden zur Liebe zwingen Kann. Aber ich moechte das Ich weiss, dass man niemanden zur Liebe zwingen Kann. Aber du solist wissen, dass ich das Gefühl habe, du bist ein Stück von mir. An dem Morgen, als du Ost-Berlin verliesst, zitterte ich am ganzen Körper. Du sagtest: Ich bin bald wieder zurück. Auch wenn ich damals nichts sagte, wusste ich sofort, dass es nie dazu kommen würde. Was nicht von Herzen kommt, geht nicht zu Herzen. Ich konnte es in deinen Augen lesen. Wenn ich hier nicht gefangen wäre, wäre ich nah beh Dir.
Du fehlst mir. Anna.

*In a slow-motion, fearful escape, **David** acts out his crossing of the Berlin Wall. He swings his upper body over, out and down, head first, holding his legs vertical above him. Gripping the wall, he swivels his* *legs down into a standing position, but remains suspended against the wall. English subtitles, projected on the wall, translate the letter:*

I know that it is impossible to force someone into loving. But you should know that I feel you are part of me. The morning you left East Berlin, I was quite shaken. You said: I'll be back soon. I did not say anything then, but I knew it would not happen that way. What does not come from the heart is not taken to heart. I could read it in your eyes. If I could leave this city, I would be with you.
I miss you. Anna.

*As the letter ends, **David** reverses his movement, until he is standing where he began the memory: in the dressing-room, behind the mirror, talking to **Lucie** who has been glided simultaneously back into her starting position. But now, **David** is crying. He wipes his eyes.*

David This stuff really burns . . . It's like getting soap in your eyes.

Lucie It won't hurt for long . . .
Sometimes you have to suffer, if you want it to look like you are suffering . . .

Gently, she wipes his eyes. The lights fade as they kiss.

Projection:
9. Apartment # 7

Interior, night.

*Stage left, a wash-basin set into the wall, with a mirror above it, indicates the bathroom in **François**' apartment. **François** enters, drunk, limping and sore. He puts his ear against the wall to listen if anyone is home next door. He calls through the wall:*

François Lucie! . . . Lucie . . .

François *puts a glass against the wall to listen for any sounds from next door.*

Silence: there is no one home. He drops his leather jacket on the floor and peels off his T-shirt. His back is marked with whiplash weals. He soaks the shirt in water and lays it across his back with a sigh of relief.

Lucie (*entering his apartment suddenly*)   François?

François   Oui ... entre. [Come in.]

Lucie   Qu'est-ce que t'as ... Es-tu malade?
[Is something wrong ... Are you sick?]

François   Oui ... J'me sens pas bien ... J'pense que j'ai trop bu ... Ça te tentes-tu de rester prendre un café?
[Yes ... I don't feel good ... I think I drank too much. D'you want to stay for a coffee?]

Lucie   Ben ... J'aimerais ça mais ... (*Pointing at the silhouette of a man waiting at the door.*) c'est parce que j'suis pas toute seule ...
[I'd like to, but uh ... I'm not alone.]

François   Ah ... Y a quelqu'un qui t'attend ...
[Ah. Someone's waiting for you.]

Lucie   Oui. On se reprendra ...
Excuses-moi de te déranger à cette heure là ... C'est parce que je viens d'arriver chez nous pis j'peux pas rentrer, j'ai pas mes clés.
[Yes. I'll take a raincheck.
Sorry to bother you so late, but I only just got home, and I can't get in. I lost my keys.]

François   Ah ...

He digs for **Lucie**'s *key inside his jeans' pocket and gives it to her.*

Lucie   Merci ... Prends soin de toi là ...
[Thank you. Well, take care ...]

As she goes to kiss him on both cheeks, she inadvertently touches his back; **François** *winces.* **Lucie** *tries to look at his back.*

Qu'est-ce que t'as, j't'ai-tu fait mal?
[What's the matter, did I hurt you?]

David (*his voice comes from behind the wall*)   Lucie? ...

François   Non, non . . . Laisse faire.
[No no . . . it's nothing.]

Lucie (*trying again to see his back*)   Ben voyons . . . Qu'est-ce
que t'as?
[Come on . . . What's the matter?]

François (*reacting violently*)   Laisse faire j'te dis . . . c'est
rien.
[Leave me alone . . . I said it's nothing!]

Lucie   OK, OK! . . .

David   Lucie, are you all right?

Lucie   Yeah, yeah . . .
(*Awkwardly, as she exits.*) Merci.

François *is now very alone. Lights cross-fade to the expanse of the
cyclorama, above the wall.*

Projection:
10. The snow

Exterior, night.

*Above the wall the moonlit night sky glows, and snow falls gently.
Music accompanies this.* **François** *appears, as if walking on the
ramparts of Quebec City's wall. He wears no shirt, only his leather
jacket, which he holds together against the cold. At one point, he stops,
climbs on to the edge of the wall, and stares down as if he's
contemplating a suicide jump. He cries silently.*

Projection:
11. Apartment # 8

Interior, day.

*Stage right, a wash-basin full of water is set into the wall, with a
mirror above it, to indicate the bathroom of* **Lucie**'*s apartment.*
David *is shaving, when he hears violent and lamenting cries from
the other side of the wall. The voice belongs to* **François**. *He checks*

*to see if **Lucie** is still sleeping, then puts his ear against the wall to listen. The cries get louder. **David** knocks on the wall a couple of times. The lamentation stops. **Lucie** enters, surprising him.*

Lucie   David, what are you doing?

David   Good morning!
Lucie, listen . . . I really have to go! I promised my secretary I'd be in Montreal at ten o'clock . . . it's now eight thirty and I haven't even left Quebec City yet. So, you can imagine how impossibly behind I am!

Lucie   That's too bad, I thought we could eat breakfast together. Shall I put on some coffee?

David   That's very nice of you, but I really must go.

Lucie   Will we see each other again?

David   Soon.

Lucie   When?

David   I have some business in Quebec City next week. Perhaps we could arrange a rendez-vous? I'll be at the morgue.

Lucie   At the morgue? I would prefer a restaurant!

She walks towards him, allowing her robe to slide from her shoulders to the ground.

David   That's what I meant . . .

*As they move into a kiss, the cries from **François'** apartment begin again. **Lucie** stops and turns her head to listen, but **David** pulls her passionately against him. As they embrace, **David** checks his watch behind her back, and figuring he has enough time, he gives in to the love scene, and lifts her up on him, turning so that she stretches out her arms to grip the wall for support as he caresses her body with his lips, and lights fade . . .*

Projection:
12. Travelling backwards[1]

Interior, day.

Thriller music begins in the blackout. Stage left, **Lucie** *stands naked, her back to the wall. Suddenly, she contracts as though she has been stabbed. She staggers forwards, and to the left, clawing at the air, then swivels as she falls: her back is covered with blood from the wall. Her movement is closely tracked by a camera on a panasonic pee-wee dolly that zooms maniacally in and out on her face and body with the tension-rhythm of the music.* **Lucie** *falls, dead, to the floor. The music stops abruptly and she gets to her feet, appearing to listen to instructions from a director. She performs three 'takes' of the death scene. After the last one, she receives the 'thumbs up' signal. She speaks to the director.*

Lucie   Can I go now?

Lucie *covers herself with a towel and exits.*

Projection:
13. The wound

Interior, night.

At **François'** *restaurant.* **David** *enters.*

François   Bonsoir, monsieur. Ce sera pour combien de personnes?

David   For two please. (*He doesn't speak French.*)

François   Does this one suit you?

David   Yes, that's fine. Oh, excuse me – would you take my coat please?

François   Sure.

[1] 'Travelling' is French film parlance for a 'dolly': smooth lateral movement of a film camera.

François *leaves with the coat. As he waits,* **David** *hides a small gift bag under his chair.*

Lucie (*entering in a rush*)   Oh, David, I'm sorry, I'm late –

David   That is perfectly fine.

Lucie   I hope you haven't been waiting too long?

David   I arrived just a moment ago. It's nice to see you.

Lucie   It was longer than I expected ... We were supposed to finish shooting at three o'clock, but we had a very complicated technical scene.

David   You look tired ...

Lucie   Playing a victim is tiring!

François (*entering to serve them*)   Bonjour, Lucie.

Lucie   Ah. Bonjour, François ... Tiens, je te présente un ami, [let me introduce you to a friend,] David Haussmann, François Tremblay ... He's my next-door neighbour ...

David   Oh ... you're the one in apartment number eight!

François   Yes.

David (*shaking his hand*)   I heard ... so much about you!

Lucie   David is the one who drove me back to Quebec City after I saw the guy throw himself in front of the train in Montreal.

François   Strange circumstances to meet someone.

David   Yes indeed ... Metro stations in Montreal seem to be used more often now to commit suicide than for commuting ...

Lucie   Why's that?

François   C'est la façon la plus cheap de se suicider ... [It's the cheapest way to kill yourself ...]

David   What?

François   ... Do you want to order something to drink before your meal?

David Well ... I think I'll avoid hard liquor –

Lucie – Me too –

David – But ... Would you like to drink some wine with the meal?

Lucie Yes ... sure.

François I'll leave you to look at the wine list. (*He gives it to* **Lucie**, *who passes it to* **David**.)

David What kind of wine do you prefer?

Lucie Well ... red or white.

David That's what I meant ... Red or white?

Lucie I like both.

David How about red?

Lucie Red? Perfect!

David What kind of red do you like ... Bourgogne, Bordeaux, Beaujolais ...

Lucie I like all of them.

David Beaujolais?

Lucie Beaujolais? Great!

David What kind of Beaujolais would you prefer?

Lucie Euh ... It's up to you!

David How about a bottle of Brouilly?

Lucie Good idea!

David Do you like Brouilly?

Lucie I love it!
You know ... it's a very good restaurant here, they serve a kind of 'mixed genre' cuisine ... A little of this ... a little of that ... French, Hindu, vegetarian ...

François (*re-entering for their order*) Have you decided on the wine?

Lucie (*scans the wine list*)   Yes, we will have a bottle of . . .
Brouilly.

François   Brouilly . . . OK.

François *exits for their order.*

David   So! How does it feel to be a movie star?

Lucie   My God, give me a chance! . . . It's my first day of
filming!
I think I felt a bit . . . silly . . . !
I found the director quite *aggressive* with his camera . . .
He wanted to shoot a scene from above, you know, as if
you're looking through the eyes of a murderer, who's
watching his victim through a skylight . . .
But during the shooting, I felt more observed by the crew,
and the director himself, than by the voyeur in the
scenario . . .

David   But aren't you used to being watched?

Lucie   In theatre, it's different. When you perform, the
audience is watching the whole you . . . But today, I felt that
they were taking me apart.

David   Taking you apart . . .

Lucie   Yes . . . Close-up of one eye, medium shot of the knife
in the back, my right hand scratching at the floor . . .

François *comes back with the bottle, shows it to* **Lucie** *who simply
reads the label.*

Lucie   Brouilly.

David   What were you filming exactly? Indoor scenes,
outdoor scenes?

Lucie   We are taking the interiors first, because the film is
set in spring . . .
So we have to wait for the end of winter.

David   What will you do if it rains all the time?

Lucie   It's a thriller! They want it to rain, because all the
scenes *happen* in the rain!

David   What if it never rains?

Lucie   Well . . . I suppose they'll make it rain!

David   Of course, just as for tears . . . As far as they are concerned, making it is not a problem, merely a question of water quantity!

Lucie   (*trying to make a pun, just as* **François** *appears with the wine*)   Exactly: when you're 'making it', it's the size of the equipment that counts!

She laughs, joined by **François** *who pours a little wine into her glass so she can 'taste' it. She is surprised not to get more.*

Merci!

François   Ben . . . Goûtes-y.

David   Taste it.

Lucie   Oh . . . yes, sure.
Hum . . . it's very good . . . (*As* **François** *pours the rest.*)
It's even a little *bouchonné*!

François   Oh – I'll get you another bottle . . .

Lucie   No no, it's very good . . . It is *bouchonné* . . . Bouchonné.

François   Yes, but . . . if it's *bouchonné* –

David   Isn't that supposed to mean that it tastes like cork?

Lucie   Well . . . in this case, it can't possibly be *bouchonné* because it tastes great!

David   Maybe I should double-check . . . It's a very expensive bottle!

David *does so, religiously. As he looks at* **François***, he seems to recognise him.*

François   Something wrong?

David   No, no . . . It's an excellent wine!

Lucie   Like I said.

François   Are you ready to order?

David   After you, Lucie.

Lucie   No, no ... You go first, David, you are the guest!

David   What do you mean, I am the guest? I thought I was the one inviting you for dinner!

Lucie   No, No ... I mean, you are the foreigner!

David (*does not respond. To* **François**)   Is this soup?

François   Yes ... Potage Crécy.

David   Well. I'll have that please, and the filet de boeuf Brisanne. I'd like that done rare but please in the French understanding of the word rare ... not the Canadian.

Lucie   I'll have the same as him, but with the Canadian rare!

François *leaves with the order.*

David   Well ... Here's to your film!

They toast. **David** *takes the package from under his chair.*

I'm not very good at this ... but here!

He puts it on the table, offering it to her.

This is for you.

Lucie   What is it?

David   What do you think it is? ... It's a present!

Lucie   But it's not my birthday.

David   It's a present just the same.

Lucie   No ... I mean ... There is no need for you to be buying me presents, David.

David   Well ... I'm sorry then.

A very awkward pause, which **Lucie** *breaks.*

Lucie   No ... No ... I'm sorry ... I'm the one acting weird here ... Let me open it!
Oh! ... A Russian doll!

David   Yes, the real thing.

Lucie   These come in all different sizes and there are people who collect them!

David   In fact . . . You won't have to collect them . . . They are all there, included one inside the other.

Lucie   What do you mean?

David   Open it!

Lucie   Oh, it's beautiful.

David   It's called a Matruska.

Lucie   A Matruska.

Lucie *opens up the dolls and lines them up on the table top so that they form a wall between her and* **David**.

David   I bought it in Eastern Europe but you find them everywhere now. It's a traditional doll. Representing generations . . . So, this big one here is the mother of this one and also the grandmother of this one because she is the mother of this one and this one is the mother of that one and that one . . . and . . . to infinity I suppose! But . . . I like to think it may stand for other things like . . . Hidden feelings. . . . One truth which is hiding another truth and another one and another one . . .

Lucie   I'm very moved . . . Thank you.

David   I'm glad you like it.

A marked 'slow' change in lights and sound indicate a time warp: time is rapidly passing. **Lucie** *and* **David** *reach for their coffee cups in slow motion, their eyes locked together.* **François** *glides in to take away the empty dishes and glasses. As he takes the bottle of wine, he slowly lays it across the middle of the table, tipping its contents so that the red wine stains the white tablecloth, and drips to the floor.*

David (*back to real time*)   . . . And at one point in the film, the angel turns to him and says:
'Beware mirrors . . . Death comes and goes through mirrors

... If you don't believe me, gaze upon yourself all your life in the looking glass and you will see her at work.'

Lucie   That's beautiful.

David   That's Cocteau.

Another time passage, marked in the same way with lights, sound and slow motion as **Lucie** *and* **David** *stir their coffee, the sounds of the spoons making an evocative late-night rhythm on their china cups.* **François** *comes in, looking at his watch. The meal has been over for a long time.*

François   I'm sorry but I am going to have to close now.

David   What time is it?

François   A quarter past three.

David   A quarter past three!

Lucie   My God! ... We didn't notice the time pass!

David   I'm very sorry ... We were completely engrossed in our conversation while digesting this excellent meal!

Lucie   Oui. Merci beaucoup ... C'était très bon.
[Yes. Thank you very much. It was very good.]

David   Can you tell me where I could find my coat please?

François   It's in the cloakroom ... I'll get it for you.

David   Lucie ... You are forgetting your Matruska!

Lucie   Oh ... my Matruska ... (*Showing it to* **François**.)
Regarde, François, ce que David m'a donné ... C'est une poupée Russe ... un Matruska. Il l'a achetée à l'Est.
[Look at what David gave to me. It's a Russian doll; a Matruska. He bought it in the East.]

François   C'est beau. [It's nice.]

They move towards the exit of the restaurant. **Lucie** *stands against the wall with the men on each side of her.* **François** *addresses* **David**.

You're from Europe?

David   Yes. I'm from East Berlin. But I have been a Canadian citizen for many years now.

François   And what do you do here?

David   I am a criminologist. I work for a criminal institution in Montreal.

François   Parthenais?

David   Yes, Parthenais.

Lucie   Tu connais ça? [You know this place?]

François   Oui ... J'ai déjà eu affaire là.
[Yes, I had to go there once.]

Lucie   Comment ça? [Why is that?]

François   Pas en prison ... I went there to undergo a polygraph test.
[Not in jail ... I went there ...]

Lucie   A what?

François   Un test de polygraphe.

David   A lie detector ... For what?

François   Because six years ago one of my best friends was murdered here in Quebec City. I was the last one to see her alive so, I was a suspect.
In fact, it was me who found her dead in her apartment. She had been tied up, raped and stabbed many times.

David   Did they find the murderer?

François   No. They never identified him.

David   What was your friend's name?

François   Marie-Claude Légaré.

Lucie *reacts to the name. As if 'flashing back' to the previous film-shoot scene, she turns as though she's been stabbed, to face the wall. Her back is covered with blood. She falls to the ground between the two men, who, without acknowledging her fall, continue to face each other in conversation.*

David   Yes ... I think I remember ... Don't worry, they'll track him down. Nobody is able to go through life with a murder on their conscience ...

As **David** *continues to talk to where he was standing,* **François** *'relives' finding his friend's corpse, kneels down by her, silently enacts his grief.*

Well, thank you once again and my compliments to the chef; the food was indeed excellent. And the service, impeccable! Have you been a waiter for long?

François *stands again to continue the conversation normally. He speaks to* **David***'s original position as* **David** *in turn kneels by* **Lucie** *and performs an 'autopsy' on her, ripping her shirt with a scalpel.*

François   Long enough ... Three years now. Before this, I was at school, university, studying Political Science – and I worked part-time in a Yugoslavian restaurant.

David   Yugoslavian ...

François   Yes. I like it better here though, it's more friendly.

David   Do you intend to do this for long? I mean ... waiting tables!
I know how transient things are in the restaurant business.

François   I don't know. If I could find work related to my studies, I'd move on for sure.

David   Well ... It's better than no work at all. You know, when I lived in East Berlin, I thought the West was full of 'golden opportunities' – but now I see how hard it is to succeed here. Over there, the jobs are trivial sometimes, but at least everybody has the right to work.

Lucie *uncoils from the floor to take the same position against the wall; simultaneously, the two men each put one foot on the wall, turning their bodies horizontal so as they appear to be in the classic cinematic 'top shot' of a corpse.* **François** *and* **David** *shake hands 'over' her body.*

David   It was a pleasure meeting you, François.

The scene returns to 'real' time and space.

Well, if we want to exercise our own right to work tomorrow, perhaps we should be moving along.

Lucie (*kisses him*)   Salut, François.

François   A bientôt, Lucie.

Lucie *walks slowly towards* **David**, *looking at her hand.*

David   What's the matter, Lucie? (*He takes her hand.*) You're bleeding!

Lucie   It's nothing. I must have cut myself with a knife.

David   Come ... We'll take care of it.

As soon as they are gone, **François** *pulls out a bag of coke, and prepares himself a few lines.*

Projection:
14. The Ramparts

Exterior, night.

A projection of the Quebec City skyscape covers the cyclorama of the theatre. **Lucie** *and* **David** *enter. She is withdrawn and quiet.*

David   What an exquisite city.

Lucie   I walk here often, but in summer usually, not winter.

David   I greatly prefer the winter. I don't know why really, but I find I like the cold ... anything cold. Perhaps it's because I was born in December. Have you noticed that when people talk about the cold, it's always in pejorative terms. But for me, the cold evokes a kind of objective calm, wisdom and above all, a great gentleness, like these snowflakes slowly falling ...
Leaning against the ramparts like that, you remind me of someone I once knew ...

Lucie   Who was she?

David   Someone whom I loved deeply and to whom I did a great wrong ... A German woman.

Lucie   I'm too nosy, aren't I?

David   It was a long time ago.
What's wrong, Lucie? Since we've left the restaurant you have seemed preoccupied somehow.

Lucie   Well ... I am. It's because – You know the story François just told us in the restaurant, about his friend? That is the story of the film we are making. It's based on the real murder situation – but I didn't know François was connected to it. It gave me a shock ...
And now I feel uneasy about playing in it, and I'm wondering if there's still time for them to find someone else.

David   They have lousy taste. To base a filmscript on an unresolved murder case ...
How do they end the movie?

Lucie   Well ... after the girl's been killed, they set everything up to look as if it was one of her close friends who did it but at the end we discover –

David   – at the end, we discover that it was the police who did it.

Lucie   How did you know?

David   It's a classic. When you don't know how to end a who-done-it, you always blame it on the cops. It's easy ...
When I was a student of criminology, I feared that the people developing investigative techniques were violent brutes: a product of their line of work. But I needn't have worried about becoming a brute.
No, they are much more dangerous than that. The men leading the field of criminal research are very, very intelligent; a fact you will never see in a thriller. It's too frightening perhaps.
Poor François ... At Parthenais they know he is innocent, but he'll probably never be told.

Lucie   Why not?

David In a police inquiry where the guilty party hasn't been identified, it's strategy to keep everyone in ignorance.

Lucie How do you know François is innocent?

David François does not know, but I was the one who conducted his polygraph test. This must remain between us, Lucie; it's a confidence.

Lucie But – how can I look him in the face without telling him?

David Stop seeing him for a while.

He tries to hold her, but she pushes him away and continues walking along the Ramparts.

Projection:
15. The call

Exterior, night.

François *enters, stage right, takes change from his pocket and crosses to stand at a phone kiosk in the stage left wing. 'Dialling a pay-phone' noises are heard.* **François** *is lit so as to blow up an enormous grotesque shadow across the entire wall, in such a way that every movement of his dialling and speaking on the phone registers. Over the phone line, we hear* **Lucie***'s answering machine.*

Lucie Bonjour, vous êtes bien chez Lucie Champagne ... Malheureusement, je ne peut pas vous répondre pour le moment mais si vous voulez bien laisser votre nom et votre numéro de téléphone, je vous rappelle dans les plus brefs délais.
[Hallo, you've reached the home of Lucie Champagne ... I'm sorry I'm not available to take your call right now, but if you leave your name and number I'll get back to you as soon as possible.]

François *lets the phone drop as the message continues. He comes back on stage, kicks the wall, then leans against it, pressing his face and body* *into it. As lights fade to black, we hear the tone of the answering machine.*

Projection:
16. The line up

Interior, night.

The line up is a re-cap scene which shows the most telling moments in the play so far. It begins with a matrix projected on the wall, reminiscent of the 'Man in Motion' photographs by Edward Muybridge.

The scene is played nude by the actors. Choreographic images of **François** *working in the restaurant,* **Lucie** *in shock in the subway,* **François** *being whipped;* **David**'s *meeting with* **Lucie**, **David** *and* **Lucie** *embracing against the wall, the 'Film Noir Top Shot' of the handshake in the restaurant. The scene and movement fragments are repeated, overlayed, dissected and recombined at a pace of increasing frenzy. Blackout.*

Projection:
17. The spring

Exterior, day.

François *has a bucket of water with which he sluices the wall. With a brush, he starts to scrub it.* **David** *enters, with sunglasses and a travel bag.*

David   Hello, François. Have you seen Lucie?

François   Not for a month, at least. She must be busy, shooting her movie.

David   I came to say goodbye, but if she is off on location ...

François   You're going away?

David   I'm going back to East Berlin. The government is sending me there for a series of conferences on investigative techniques. Now that the Wall has disappeared, there is a great demand for up-to-date technologies. But to tell you the truth, my motivation is more personal than professional.

François   And what's the government's motivation: to share knowledge or sell free enterprise?

David   To share knowledge.
Well, if you see Lucie, tell her I was here . . .

He makes as if to leave, then stops.

What the hell are you doing, François?

François   I'm washing the wall.

David   Yes, I can see, but why?

François   The landlord told me to strip my graffiti off the garden wall before I move out, or else he'll prosecute.

David   Prosecute . . . For graffiti! . . . What did it say?

François   L'histoire s'écrit avec le sang.

David   Which means?

François   'History is written with blood.'
It means that we write history through war, fascism and murder.

David   Murder . . . You mean political assassinations.

François   No. I mean murders. The smallest little killing, of some totally unimportant person . . . In a way that's still a political act, don't you think?

David   Is that what you learned in political sciences?

François *loses his temper.*

François   Why do you ask me so many questions? You sound like an interrogator in a bad detective movie?

Defiantly, **François** *gathers up his bucket and brush, and exits.*

Projection:
18. Travelling forwards[2]

Exterior, night.

Lucie *appears in profile, stage left, behind and above the wall. She's lit from behind by the light of a movie projector positioned in the stage left wing. The rushes of the movie are projected onto the stage right wall, but are not visible to the audience. While she is watching the rushes of the movie the projector stops.*

Lucie (*addressing the director offstage*)   This is from yesterday? And what we shoot tomorrow will be linked with it – ?

She starts to cry silently.

– Excuse me . . .

She pulls herself together.

May I see it again please?

Blackout.

Projection:
19. Apartment # 8

Interior, day.

François *is packing boxes in the washroom of his apartment. The wash-basin is set into the wall as before.* **Lucie** *enters with books.*

The scene is translated into subtitles that are projected with slides on the wall.

Lucie   Salut, François, je t'ai rapporté les livres que tu m'avais prêté . . . L'orgasme au masculin, j'ai trouvé ça ben intéressant.
[Hi, François. I brought back the books you lent me; I found *The Male Orgasm* pretty interesting.]

François   Tu peux les garder encore si t'as pas fini.
[You can keep them if you're not finished.]

[2] Dolly in

Lucie Non, non ... je sais ce que je voulais savoir ...
[No, no ... I found out everything I wanted to know!]

She examines the cosmetics strewn in the wash-basin.

Ouan ... t'en a des affaires pour un gars ...
[You got a lot of make-up for a guy ...]

She starts to poke around in one of his boxes as he puts the books in.

T'écris pas ce que tu mets dans tes boites?
[You don't write what you put into the boxes?]

François C'est pas nécessaire ... Pour ce que j'ai ...
[There's no point. I haven't got much stuff.]

Lucie Ecris au moins où est ce que ça va, sinon tu vas être
mêlé quand tu vas arriver là-bas.
[You should at least write where it goes, so you won't be
mixed up when you move to your new place.]

Pointing to a box.

Ca c'est quoi? Des cosmétiques? Je vais écrire pharmacie
dessus. Pis celle-là?
[What is in there? Cosmetics? I'll write 'personal things' on
the side. And what's in this one?]

François Là dedans ... des couvertures, serviettes des
débarbouillettes, des livres, des vieux journaux ...
[Blankets, facecloths, books, old newspapers ...]

Lucie J'pourrais écrire divers.
[I could write ... miscellaneous.]

Inside the box, **Lucie** *finds a long leather strap with a strange
fastening at the end.*

Ca, ça sert à quoi? [And – What is this used for?]

François (*puts the strap around his neck and demonstrates*)
Quand je me masturbe, je me sers de ça. Je tire – puis je lâche,
je tire – pis je lâche. Puis, juste avant de venir, je tire de plus
en plus fort ... Mais à un moment donné, il faut qu'tu lâches,
si tu veux pas venir pour la dernière fois.
[I use it when I masturbate. I pull then release, pull and

release and just before I come, I pull harder and harder . . .
There's a certain point where I have to let go, or else it'll be
the last time I come.]

Lucie   Est-ce que ça sert juste à ça?
[Is that all you use it for?]

François *takes the strap from around his neck and goes to the wash-
basin.*

François   Viens ici. [Come here.]

She hesitates.

Viens ici! [Come here!]

She does.

Assied-toi, donnes-moi ta main.
[Sit down; give me your hand.]

He ties the belt around **Lucie***'s hand, takes it through the U-bend pipe
on the wash-basin and wraps it round her neck before tying it up.*

In a simultaneous scene, **David** *gives a lecture about the polygraph
machine in East Berlin. He stands upstage of the wall, but not above it.
He is visible to the audience only as a reflection in the two-way mirror
which is positioned at such an angle as to reveal him.*

David   . . . Firstly, the lie registers on the *cardiograph*, with
an accelerated heartbeat. At the *temple*, we monitor for an
increase or, in the case of some subjects, a decrease of arterial
pressure –

François   Là je vais serrer un peu . . .
[I'm going to tighten it a bit . . .]

David   *Respiration* has a direct effect on the person
responding to questions: this contributes yet another reading
of the physical response. Lastly, we measure the subject's
perspiration. The polygraph machine detects the most minute
psycho-physical variations occuring during interrogation.

François *puts a blindfold on her eyes, rendering her completely
helpless.*

François   Comme ça, t'as vraiment l'impression d'être vulnérable...
[This makes you feel really vulnerable...]

David   The fear and mystique which surrounds the polygraph machine, makes it a useful pressure tactic in obtaining a confession. But such strategies, I believe, should be used only with great care and compassion. Sometimes, the psychological response we trigger is so violent as to effect a lasting disorder in the mind of a totally innocent suspect.

Lucie   Pis après? [And then?]

David   Let me tell you about a polygraph test undertaken in the context of an unresolved murder case. The questioning of a particular suspect went somewhat like this:

François   Des fois, quand on se ramasse une gang de gars...
[Sometimes, when I get together with a gang of friends...]

David   François, we are going to conduct a little test.

François   Y'en a un qui se fait attacher comme ça...
[One of us gets tied up like this...]

David   Can you hear me properly?

François   ...Pis au hasard y'en a un autre qui est choisi pour aller le rejoindre...
[...Then someone is picked at random to go in and join him...]

David   But you cannot actually see me can you?

François   ...celui qui est attaché, il peut rien faire...
[...the one who's all tied up can't do anything...]

David   François, are we in Canada?

François   ...il peut rien voir...
[...he can't see anything...]

David   Is it summertime?

François   ...pis l'autre il fait ce qu'il veut avec...
[...and the other one does whatever he wants with him.]

David Was it you who killed Marie-Claude Légaré?

François (*in his memory, he 're-lives' the polygraph test scene*) Non.

David Is it 1986?

François Oui.

David Are we in the month of August?

François Non.

David Is it the month of July?

François Oui.

David Are you responsible for the death of Marie-Claude Légaré?

François Non.

David Now, the result of this polygraph test gave evidence that this witness was actually telling the truth. But the person conducting the test told him afterwards that the machine had established that the test was inconclusive: so as to consider the spontaneous reaction of the witness as the ultimate proof of his innocence . . .

François (*a complete emotional breakdown*) Allez-vous me lâcher tabarnak! C'est pas moi qui l'a tuée!! C'est pas moi!! Vous voulez me rendre fou, c'est ça!! Y vont me rendre fou hostie . . .
[Let me fucking go! I didn't kill her!! It wasn't me! It wasn't me! You want to drive me mad, that's it!! You are driving me mad, Christ . . .]

Lucie François . . . ?
François . . . ?
François?

David But the police never told him he was released from suspicion . . .
He was never let off the hook.

François *slowly recovers, goes to her and takes off the blindfold.*

François Veux-tu que je te détache?
[Do you want me to untie you?]

He does so, then silently puts the belt and blindfold in a box.

Lucie Est-ce que c'est toi qui l'a tuée?
[Was it you killed her?]

François ...J'pense pas non... [I don't think so ...]

Lucie Pourquoi tu dis 'j'pense' pas?
[Why do you say ... You don't 'think' so?]

François Parce que des fois... je l'sais plus.
[Because sometimes ... I don't know any more.]

He starts to cry, an emotion from deep inside. **Lucie** *goes to him, takes him in her arms.*

Lucie Moi, je l'sais ... que tu serais pas capable de faire mal à une mouche.
[Listen ... I know: I know that you couldn't hurt a fly.]

She holds him, fiercely comforting and reassuring him. She touches his face, and the comfort becomes passion. Lights fade as they start to embrace.

Projection:
20. The rain

Exterior, day.

Rain falls from the ceiling behind the wall. Above the wall the camera appears, covered with an umbrella. **Lucie** *has not turned up for the day's filming.*

Projection:
21. Apartment # 7

Interior, night.

An eerie dream sequence. **Lucie** *leans against the wall with a hidden light strapped to her back. It shines at the wall, creating a strange halo around her body, and placing her in silhouette. She walks slowly to the front of the stage.*

David (*entering stage left*)   Lucie! I'm back!

François *enters from* **Lucie**'s *bedroom, without a shirt.* **David** *is shocked. He appears not to see* **Lucie** *downstage, and speaks to* **François** *behind her back.*

What are you doing here? Where's Lucie?

François   She's in the room.

David *goes in to the room then comes back in anger.*

David (*showing the exit*)   Get out!

François   Maybe we could talk . . .

David   Get out!

François   Wait . . .

David *seizes* **François** *to throw him out, and they fight violently.* **François**' *head is knocked against the wall. Slowly,* **Lucie** *walks backwards to her original place, and the lighting changes. She leans against the wall, lost in her thoughts.* **François** *enters from the bedroom. He leans against the wall beside* **Lucie**. *He is restless and anxious. They smile gently at one another, and* **François** *takes her hand, as if unable to speak the things in his heart. He holds her like a frightened child – which then becomes a passionate kiss.* **François** *then withdraws, and bids goodbye to* **Lucie**. *He exits.*

David's *voice is heard offstage.*

David   Lucie! I'm back!

He enters.

How are you?

Lucie I'm fine . . .

David *takes his bag into the bedroom, then comes back and starts to wash his face in the washbasin.*

David I thought you were supposed to be filming today?

Lucie Yes . . . I was scheduled, but I decided not to go.

David Why?

Lucie We were scheduled to shoot the close-ups for the death sequence, and I feel I have no right to do it.

David This is very courageous of you.

Lucie François just left for Montreal . . .
David . . . While you were away – I slept with François.

David *stops washing, abruptly. He holds very still.*

Lucie I've spent the whole week with him because he needed someone. And I told him everything you told me on the ramparts. He told you the truth, but you lied to him.

She looks at **David**, *who has straightened to regard her, without expression.*

David . . . React! . . . Feel something!

David (*as he calmly turns to her*) What do you want me to 'feel'? You want me to be jealous of a fucking homosexual?

Lucie If that's the truth, yes!
If you want to cry, cry!

The lights fade on them.

Projection:
22. Death

Interior, night.

Behind the wall, **François** *arrives at the Metro station and paces impatiently, waiting for the train. We can't see him but he is lit so that his silhouette is projected upon the cyclorama behind the wall.*

Lucie *appears above the wall to perform Hamlet. She holds a knife and recites the famous soliloquy as* **François** *waits.*

Lucie   Etre ou ne pas être, c'est là la question.
Est-il plus noble de subir la fronde et les
flèches de la fortune outrageante, ou bien
à s'armer contre une mer de douleurs et à
l'arrêter par une révolte? Mourir,
... dormir, rien de plus; ... Et dire que par ce
sommeil nous mettrons fin aux maux du
coeur et aux mille tortures naturelles qui
sont le lot de la chair: c'est là un
dénouement qu'on doit souhaiter avec
ferveur. Mourir ... dormir, dormir! peut-
être rêver! Oui, là est l'embarras. Car
quels rêves peut-il nous venir dans ce
sommeil de la mort, quand nous sommes
dépouillés de cette enveloppe charnelle?
Voilà qui doit nous arrêter. C'est cette
réflexion là qui nous vaut la calamité
d'une si longue vie.
[To be, or not to be – that is the question;
Whether 'tis nobler in the mind to suffer
The slings and arrows of outrageous fortune
Or to take arms agains a sea of troubles
And by opposing end them. To die, to sleep –
No more – and by a sleep to say we end
The heartache and the thousand natural shocks
That flesh is heir to. 'Tis a consummation
Devoutly to be wished. To die, to sleep –
To sleep – perchance to dream. Ay, there's the rub.
For in that sleep of death what dreams may come
When we have shuffled off this mortal coil
Must give us pause. There's the respect
That makes calamity of so long life.]

The lights on her fade slowly. We hear the sound of the train coming.
François *takes off his leather jacket and lets it fall to the floor behind him; without hesitation, he throws himself in front of the arriving train. As his silhouette dives out of sight, the brick wall suddenly falls*

and a piercing light shines through as **François'** *naked body comes hurtling through the falling bricks to land on a hospital trolley. There he lies, amidst the broken bricks, dead and awaiting an autopsy.*
David *pushes the trolley stage right, so that it is positioned beneath the mirror, which is hung at an angle such that* **François'** *body is reflected in it. Slowly, the reflection in the mirror over him changes so that we no longer see his body, but a skeleton, which lies in the same position, as if the mirror sees through his flesh.*

Above the wall, across the cyclorama, clouds are running in a vast sky.

Methuen Modern Plays

include work by

Edward Albee
Jean Anouilh
John Arden
Margaretta D'Arcy
Peter Barnes
Sebastian Barry
Brendan Behan
Dermot Bolger
Edward Bond
Bertolt Brecht
Howard Brenton
Anthony Burgess
Simon Burke
Jim Cartwright
Caryl Churchill
Noël Coward
Lucinda Coxon
Sarah Daniels
Nick Darke
Nick Dear
Shelagh Delaney
David Edgar
David Eldridge
Dario Fo
Michael Frayn
John Godber
Paul Godfrey
David Greig
John Guare
Peter Handke
David Harrower
Jonathan Harvey
Iain Heggie
Declan Hughes
Terry Johnson
Sarah Kane
Charlotte Keatley
Barrie Keeffe
Howard Korder

Robert Lepage
Doug Lucie
Martin McDonagh
John McGrath
Terrence McNally
David Mamet
Patrick Marber
Arthur Miller
Mtwa, Ngema & Simon
Tom Murphy
Phyllis Nagy
Peter Nichols
Sean O'Brien
Joseph O'Connor
Joe Orton
Louise Page
Joe Penhall
Luigi Pirandello
Stephen Poliakoff
Franca Rame
Mark Ravenhill
Philip Ridley
Reginald Rose
Willy Russell
Jean-Paul Sartre
Sam Shepard
Wole Soyinka
Shelagh Stephenson
Peter Straughan
C. P. Taylor
Theatre de Complicite
Theatre Workshop
Sue Townsend
Judy Upton
Timberlake Wertenbaker
Roy Williams
Snoo Wilson
Victoria Wood

Methuen World Classics

include

Jean Anouilh (two volumes)
Lorca (three volumes)
John Arden (two volumes)
Marivaux
Arden & D'Arcy
Mustapha Matura
Brendan Behan
David Mercer (two volumes)
Aphra Behn
Arthur Miller (five volumes)
Bertolt Brecht (eight volumes)
Molière
Büchner
Musset
Bulgakov
Peter Nichols (two volumes)
Calderón
Joe Orton
Čapek
A. W. Pinero
Anton Chekhov

Luigi Pirandello
Noël Coward (eight volumes)
Terence Rattigan
Feydean
(two volumes)
Eduardo De Filippo
W. Somerset Maughan
Max Frisch
(two volumes)
John Galsworthy
August Strindberg
Gogol
(three volumes)
Gorky
J. M. Synge
Harley Granville Barker
Ramón del Valle-Inclán
    (two volumes)
Frank Wedekind
Henrik Ibsen (six volumes)
Oscar Wilde

Methuen Student Editions

Jean Anouilh	*Antigone*
John Arden	*Serjeant Musgrave's Dance*
Alan Ayckbourn	*Confusions*
Aphra Behn	*The Rover*
Edward Bond	*Lear*
Bertolt Brecht	*The Caucasian Chalk Circle*
	Life of Galileo
	Mother Courage and her Children
	The Resistible Rise of Arturo Ui
Anton Chekhov	*The Cherry Orchard*
	The Seagull
	The Three Sisters
Caryl Churchill	*Serious Money*
	Top Girls
Shelagh Delaney	*A Taste of Honey*
Euripides	*Medea*
Dario Fo	*Accidental Death of an Anarchist*
Michael Frayn	*Copenhagen*
John Galsworthy	*Strife*
Nikolai Gogol	*The Government Inspector*
Robert Holman	*Across Oka*
Henrik Ibsen	*A Doll's House*
	Hedda Gabler
Charlotte Keatley	*My Mother Said I Never Should*
Bernard Kops	*Dreams of Anne Frank*
Federico García Lorca	*Blood Wedding*
	The House of Bernarda Alba
	(bilingual edition)
Willy Russell	*Blood Brothers*
Wole Soyinka	*Death and the King's Horseman*
August Strindberg	*The Father*
J. M. Synge	*The Playboy of the Western World*
Oscar Wilde	*The Importance of Being Earnest*
Tennessee Williams	*A Streetcar Named Desire*
	The Glass Menagerie
Timberlake Wertenbaker	*Our Country's Good*